Writing Idiomatic Python

Jeff Knupp

2013

Jeff Knupp Visit me at www.jeffknupp.com

Preface

There's a famous old quote about writing maintainable software:

```
Always code as if the guy who ends up maintaining your code
will be a violent psychopath who knows where you live.
--John Woods comp.lang.c++
```

While I'm not usually one for aphorisms, this one strikes a chord with me. Maybe it's because I've spent my professional career writing software at huge companies, but I have yet to inherit code that didn't eventually cause me to curse the original author at some point. Everyone (besides you, of course, dear reader) struggles to write code that's easy to maintain. When Python became popular, many thought that, because of its terseness, it would naturally lead to more maintainable software.

Alas, maintainability is not an emergent property of using an expressive language. Badly written Python code is just as unmaintainable as badly written C++, Perl, Java and all the rest of the languages known for their, *ahem*, readability. Terse code is not a free lunch.

So what do we do? Resign ourselves to maintaining code we can't understand? Rant on Twitter and The Daily WTF about the awful code we have to work on? What must we do to stop the pain?

Write. Idiomatic. Code.

It's that simple. Idioms in a programming language are a sort of lingua franca to let future readers know exactly what we're trying to accomplish. We may document our code extensively, write exhaustive unit tests, and hold code reviews three times a day, but the fact remains: when someone else needs to make changes, the code is king. If that someone is you, all the documentation in the world won't help you understand unreadable code. After all, how can you even be sure the code is doing what the documentation says?

We're usually reading someone else's code because there's a problem. But idiomatic code helps here, too. Even if it's wrong, when code is written idiomatically, it's far easier to spot bugs. Idiomatic code reduces the cognitive load on the reader. After learning a language's idioms, you'll spend less time wondering ``Wait, why are they using a named tuple there'' and more time understanding what the code actually does.

After you learn and internalize a language's idioms, reading the code of a like-minded developer feels like speed reading. You're no longer stopping at every line, trying to figure out what it does while struggling to keep in mind what came before. Instead, you'll find yourself almost skimming the code, thinking things like `OK, open a file, transform the contents to a sorted list, generate the giant report in a thread-safe way.' When you have that level of insight into code someone else wrote, there's no bug you can't fix and no enhancement you can't make.

All of this sounds great, right? There's only one catch: you have to know and use a language's idioms to benefit. Enter Writing Idiomatic Python. What started as a hasty blog post of idioms (fueled largely by my frustration while fixing the code of experienced developers new to Python) is now a full-fledged eBook.

I hope you find the book useful. It is meant to be a living document, updated in near-real time with corrections, clarifications, and additions. If you find an error in the text or have difficulty deciphering a passage, please feel free to email me at jeff@jeffknupp.com. With their permission, I'll be adding the names of all who contribute bug fixes and clarifications to the appendix.

Cheers,

Jeff Knupp

January, 2013

Change List

Version 1.1, February 2, 2013

- **New idiom:** ``Use `sys.exit` in your script to return proper error codes" idiom
- Greatly expanded discussion in ``Avoid comparing directly to True, False, or None" and added mention of comparison to None when checking if optional arguments were set (to match the idiom ``Avoid using '', [], and {} as default parameters to functions".
- Expanded ``Use the `* operator` to represent the"rest" of a list" idiom expanded with additional cases
- Fixed page numbering issue causing numbers in table of contents and index not to match the text
- Fixed various typos and grammatical errors
- Changed font size and various layout issues (some of which caused text to run off the page
- Changed preface text

Version 1.2, February 17, 2013

- Improved formatting for epub and Kindle versions
- Fixed various typos and grammatical errors

Version 1.3, June 16, 2013

- **3 New Sections: Exceptions, Testing, Documentation**
    - These will be expanded in future versions
- **New Idiom:** ``Use a `dict` as a substitute for a `switch...case` statement"
- **Python 2.7+ New Idiom:** ``Use the function-based version of `print`"
    - Previously, the use of `print()` as a function in the Python 2.7+ edition code samples was a source of confusion as the `import` statement enabling it was omitted for brevity

- ``Conventions'' section outlining a number of conventions used in the book. Specifically, those listed were identified by readers as a source of confusion.
- **11 new idioms and 3 new sections in total**

Version 1.4, November 22, 2013

- **New Idiom:** ``Make use of **init**.py files to simplify package interfaces''
- **New Idiom:** ``Use namedtuples to make tuple-heave code more clear''
- **New Idiom:** ``Use properties to future-proof your classes''
- **Rewritten Idiom**: ``Avoid '', [], and {} as default parameters to functions'' was rewritten for both correctness and clarity
- Improved formatting for all versions
- Fixed various typos and grammatical errors

Conventions

This book adopts a number of conventions for convenience and readability purposes. Two in particular bear mentioning explicitly to clear up any confusion:

- `print()` is used as a function in both editions of the book. In the 2.7+ edition, there is an idiom devoted to using print in this way through the statement `from __future__ import print_function`. In all other code samples, this import statement is omitted for brevity.
- In some code samples, PEP-8 and/or PEP-257 are violated to accomodate formatting limitations or for brevity. In particular, most functions in code samples do not contain docstrings. Here again, the book has an explicit idiom regarding the consistent use of docstrings; they are ommitted for brevity. This may change in future versions
- All code samples, if they were part of a stand-alone script, would include an `if __name__ == '__main__'` statement and a `main()` function, as described by the idioms ``Use the `if __name__ == '__main__'` pattern to allow a file to be both imported and run directly'' and ``Use `sys.exit` in your script to return proper error codes''. These statements are ommitted in code samples for brevity.

Contents

Chapter 1

Control Structures and Functions

1.1 If Statements

1.1.1 Avoid placing conditional branch code on the same line as the colon

Using indentation to indicate scope (like you already do everywhere else in Python) makes it easy to determine what will be executed as part of a conditional statement. `if`, `elif`, and `else` statements should always be on their own line. No code should follow the `:`.

1.1.1.1 Harmful

```python
name = 'Jeff'
address = 'New York, NY'

if name: print(name)
print(address)
```

1.1.1.2 Idiomatic

```python
name = 'Jeff'
address = 'New York, NY'

if name:
    print(name)
print(address)
```

1.1.2 Avoid repeating variable name in compound `if` statement

When one wants to check a variable against a number of values, repeatedly listing the variable being checked is unnecessarily verbose. Using an `iterable` makes the code more clear and improves readability.

1.1.2.1 Harmful

```python
is_generic_name = False
name = 'Tom'
if name == 'Tom' or name == 'Dick' or name == 'Harry':
    is_generic_name = True
```

1.1.2.2 Idiomatic

```python
name = 'Tom'
is_generic_name = name in ('Tom', 'Dick', 'Harry')
```

1.1.3 Avoid comparing directly to **True**, **False**, or **None**

For any object, be it a built-in or user defined, there is a ``truthiness'' associated with the object. When checking if a condition is true, prefer relying on the implicit ``truthiness'' of the object in the conditional statement. The rules regarding ``truthiness'' are reasonably straightforward. All of the following are considered `False`:

- `None`
- `False`
- zero for numeric types
- empty sequences
- empty dictionaries
- a value of `0` or `False` returned when either `__len__` or `__nonzero__` is called

Everything else is considered `True` (and thus most things are implicitly `True`). The last condition for determining `False`, by checking the value returned by `__len__` or `__nonzero__`, allows you to define how ``truthiness'' should work for any class you create.

`if` statements in Python make use of ``truthiness'' implicitly, and you should too. Instead of checking if a variable `foo` is `True` like this

```python
if foo == True:
```

you should simply check `if foo:`.

There are a number of reasons for this. The most obvious is that if your code changes and `foo` becomes an `int` instead of `True` or `False`, your `if` statement still works. But at a deeper level, the reasoning is based on the difference between `equality` and `identity`. Using `==` determines if two objects have the same value (as defined by their `_eq` attribute). Using `is` determines if the two objects are *actually the same object*.

Note that while there are cases where `is` works as if it were comparing for equality, these are special cases and shouldn't be relied upon.

As a consequence, avoid comparing directly to `False` and `None` and empty sequences like `[]`, `{}`, and `()`. If a list named `my_list` is empty, calling `if my_list:` will evaluate to `False`.

There *are* times, however, when comparing directly to `None` is not just recommended, but required. A function checking if an argument whose default value is `None` was actually set must compare directly to `None` like so:

```python
def insert_value(value, position=None):
    """Inserts a value into my container, optionally at the
```

```
    specified position"""
    if position is not None:
        ...
```

What's wrong with `if position:`? Well, if someone wanted to insert into position 0, the function would act as if position hadn't been set, since 0 evaluates to `False`. Note the use of `is not`: comparisons against None (a singleton in Python) should always use `is` or `is not`, not == (from PEP8).

Just let Python's ``truthiness" do the work for you.

1.1.3.1 Harmful

```python
def number_of_evil_robots_attacking():
    return 10


def should_raise_shields():
    # "We only raise Shields when one or more giant robots attack,
    # so I can just return that value..."
    return number_of_evil_robots_attacking()

if should_raise_shields() == True:
    raise_shields()
    print('Shields raised')
else:
    print('Safe! No giant robots attacking')
```

1.1.3.2 Idiomatic

```python
def number_of_evil_robots_attacking():
    return 10


def should_raise_shields():
    # "We only raise Shields when one or more giant robots attack,
    # so I can just return that value..."
    return number_of_evil_robots_attacking()

if should_raise_shields():
    raise_shields()
    print('Shields raised')
```

```python
else:
    print('Safe! No giant robots attacking')
```

1.2 For loops

1.2.1 Use the **enumerate** function in loops instead of creating an ``index" variable

Programmers coming from other languages are used to explicitly declaring a variable to track the index of a container in a loop. For example, in C++:

```cpp
for (int i=0; i < container.size(); ++i)
{
    // Do stuff
}
```

In Python, the enumerate built-in function handles this role.

1.2.1.1 Harmful

```python
my_container = ['Larry', 'Moe', 'Curly']
index = 0
for element in my_container:
    print ('{} {}'.format(index, element))
    index += 1
```

1.2.1.2 Idiomatic

```python
my_container = ['Larry', 'Moe', 'Curly']
for index, element in enumerate(my_container):
    print ('{} {}'.format(index, element))
```

1.2.2 Use the `in` keyword to iterate over an `iterable`

Programmers coming from languages lacking a `for_each` style construct are used to iterating over a container by accessing elements via index. Python's `in` keyword handles this gracefully.

1.2.2.1 Harmful

```python
my_list = ['Larry', 'Moe', 'Curly']
index = 0
while index < len(my_list):
    print (my_list[index])
    index += 1
```

1.2.2.2 Idiomatic

```python
my_list = ['Larry', 'Moe', 'Curly']
for element in my_list:
    print (element)
```

1.2.3   Use **else** to execute code after a **for** loop concludes

One of the lesser known facts about Python's for loop is that it can include an else clause. The else clause is executed after the iterator is exhausted, unless the loop was ended prematurely due to a break statement. This allows you to check for a condition in a for loop, break if the condition holds for an element, else take some action if the condition did not hold for any of the elements being looped over. This obviates the need for conditional flags in a loop solely used to determine if some condition held.

In the scenario below, we are running a report to check if any of the email addresses our users registered are malformed (users can register multiple addresses).   The idiomatic version is more concise thanks to not having to deal with the has_malformed_email_address flag. What's more, *even if another programmer wasn't familiar with the* for ... else *idiom, our code is clear enough to teach them.*

1.2.3.1   Harmful

```python
for user in get_all_users():
    has_malformed_email_address = False
    print ('Checking {}'.format(user))
    for email_address in user.get_all_email_addresses():
        if email_is_malformed(email_address):
            has_malformed_email_address = True
            print ('Has a malformed email address!')
            break
    if not has_malformed_email_address:
        print ('All email addresses are valid!')
```

1.2.3.2   Idiomatic

```python
for user in get_all_users():
    print ('Checking {}'.format(user))
    for email_address in user.get_all_email_addresses():
        if email_is_malformed(email_address):
            print ('Has a malformed email address!')
            break
    else:
        print ('All email addresses are valid!')
```

1.3 Functions

1.3.1 Avoid using a mutable object as the `default value` for a function argument

When the Python interpreter encouters a function definition, default arguments are evaulated to determine their value. This evaluation, however, occurs only once. *Calling* the function does not trigger another evaluation of the arguments. Since the computed
value is used in all subsequent calls to the function, using a mutable object as a default value often yields unintended results.

A *mutable* object is one whose value can be changed directly. `list`, `dict`, `set`, and most class instances are mutable. We can
mutate a `list` by calling `append` on it. The object has been changed to contain the `appended` element.

Immutable objects, by contrast, can not be altered after they are created. `string`, `int`, and `tuple` objects are all examples
of immutable objects. We can't directly change the value of a `string`, for example. All `string` operations that would alter a
`string` instead return *new* `string` objects.

So why does this matter for default arguments? Recall that the value initially computed for a default arugment is reused each time
the function is called. For immutable objects like `strings`, this is fine, since there is no way for us to change that value directly.
For mutable objects, however, changing the value of a default argument will be reflected in subsequent calls to the function. In the
example below (taken from the offical Python tutorial), an empty `list` is used as a default argument value. If the function adds an
element to that `list`, *the `list` argument will still contain that element the next time the function is called*. The `list` argument
is not ``reset'' to an empty list; rather, the same `list` object is used for every call to that function.

1.3.1.1 Harmful

```python
def f(a, L=[]):
    L.append(a)
    return L

print(f(1))
print(f(2))
print(f(3))

# This will print
#
# [1]
# [1, 2]
# [1, 2, 3]
```

1.3.1.2 Idiomatic

```python
# If you don't want the default to be shared between subsequent
# calls, you can write the function like this instead:

def f(a, L=None):
    if L is None:
        L = []
    L.append(a)
    return L

print(f(1))
print(f(2))
print(f(3))

# This will print
# [1]
# [2]
# [3]
```

1.3.2   Use `*args` and `**kwargs` to accept arbitrary arguments

Oftentimes, functions need to accept an arbitrary list of `positional parameters` and/or `keyword parameters`, use a subset of them, and forward the rest to another function. Using `*args` and `**kwargs` as parameters allows a function to accept an arbitrary list of positional and keyword arguments, respectively.

The idiom is also useful when maintaining backwards compatibility in an API. If our function accepts arbitrary arguments, we are free to add new arguments in a new version while not breaking existing code using fewer arguments. As long as everything is properly documented, the ``actual'' parameters of a function are not of much consequence.

Of course, that's not to say that we should simply stop using named parameters in functions. Indeed, this should be our default. There are, however, a number of situations where the use of `*args` and `**kwargs` is useful or necessary.

1.3.2.1   Harmful

```python
def make_api_call(foo, bar, baz):
    if baz in ('Unicorn', 'Oven', 'New York'):
        return foo(bar)
    else:
        return bar(foo)

# I need to add another parameter to `make_api_call`
# without breaking everyone's existing code.
# I have two options...

def so_many_options():
    # I can tack on new parameters, but only if I make
    # all of them optional...
    def make_api_call(foo, bar, baz, qux=None, foo_polarity=None,
                      baz_coefficient=None, quux_capacitor=None,
                      bar_has_hopped=None, true=None, false=None,
                      file_not_found=None):
        # ... and so on ad infinitum
        return file_not_found

def version_graveyard():
    # ... or I can create a new function each time the signature
    # changes.
    def make_api_call_v2(foo, bar, baz, qux):
```

```python
        return make_api_call(foo, bar, baz) - qux

    def make_api_call_v3(foo, bar, baz, qux, foo_polarity):
        if foo_polarity != 'reversed':
            return make_api_call_v2(foo, bar, baz, qux)
        return None

    def make_api_call_v4(
            foo, bar, baz, qux, foo_polarity, baz_coefficient):
        return make_api_call_v3(
            foo, bar, baz, qux, foo_polarity) * baz_coefficient

    def make_api_call_v5(
            foo, bar, baz, qux, foo_polarity,
            baz_coefficient, quux_capacitor):
        # I don't need 'foo', 'bar', or 'baz' anymore, but I have to
        # keep supporting them...
        return baz_coefficient * quux_capacitor

    def make_api_call_v6(
            foo, bar, baz, qux, foo_polarity, baz_coefficient,
            quux_capacitor, bar_has_hopped):
        if bar_has_hopped:
            baz_coefficient *= -1
        return make_api_call_v5(foo, bar, baz, qux,
                                foo_polarity, baz_coefficient,
                                quux_capacitor)

    def make_api_call_v7(
            foo, bar, baz, qux, foo_polarity, baz_coefficient,
            quux_capacitor, bar_has_hopped, true):
        return true

    def make_api_call_v8(
            foo, bar, baz, qux, foo_polarity, baz_coefficient,
            quux_capacitor, bar_has_hopped, true, false):
        return false
```

```python
def make_api_call_v9(
        foo, bar, baz, qux, foo_polarity, baz_coefficient,
        quux_capacitor, bar_has_hopped,
        true, false, file_not_found):
    return file_not_found
```

1.3.2.2   Idiomatic

```python
def make_api_call(foo, bar, baz):
    if baz in ('Unicorn', 'Oven', 'New York'):
        return foo(bar)
    else:
        return bar(foo)


# I need to add another parameter to `make_api_call`
# without breaking everyone's existing code.
# Easy...


def new_hotness():
    def make_api_call(foo, bar, baz, *args, **kwargs):
        # Now I can accept any type and number of arguments
        # without worrying about breaking existing code.
        baz_coefficient = kwargs['the_baz']

        # I can even forward my args to a different function without
        # knowing their contents!
        return baz_coefficient in new_function(args)
```

1.3.3 Use the function-based version of `print`

In Python 3.0, `print` was changed from a special language construct to a normal built-in function. The reasons for the change are listed in PEP 3105, summarized in the list below:

- There is nothing about `print` that requires special language syntax
- Replacing `print` with an alternative implementation is often desirable, but difficult if `print` is language syntax
- Converting `print` calls to use a separator other than spaces is difficult at best.

Python 2.6 included a mechanism for using the new `print()` function by including it in Python's standard mechanism for back-porting changes from Python 3 to Python 2: the `__future__` module. For both the reasons listed above and, more importantly, to make transitioning your code from Python 2 to 3 as easy as possible, using the function-based `print` is recommended.

1.3.3.1 Harmful

```python
print 1, 'foo', __name__
```

1.3.3.2 Idiomatic

```python
from __future__ import print_function
print(1, 'foo', __name__)
```

1.4 Exceptions

1.4.1 Don't be Afraid to Use Exceptions

In many languages, exceptions are reserved for truly exceptional cases. For example, a function that takes a file name as an argument and performs some calculations on the file's contents probably shouldn't throw an exception if the file is not found. That's not too ``exceptional''; it's probably a reasonably common occurrence. If, however, the file system itself were unavailable, raising an exception makes sense.

Because (in other languages) deciding when to raise an exception is partly a matter of taste (and thus experience), novices tend to overuse them. This overuse of exceptions leads to a number of problems: the control flow of a program is more difficult to follow, they create a burden on calling code when allowed to propagate up a call chain, and in many languages they impose a stiff performance penalty. These facts have led to a general vilification of exceptions. Many organizations have explicit coding standards that forbid their use (see, for example, Google's official C++ Style Guide).

Python takes a different view. Exceptions can be found in almost every popular third-party package, and the Python standard library makes liberal use of them. In fact, exceptions are built into fundamental parts of the language itself. For example, did you know that any time you use a for loop in Python, you're using exceptions?

That may sound odd, but it's true: exceptions are used for control flow throughout the Python language. Have you ever wondered how for loops know when to stop? For things like lists that have an easily determined length the question seems trivial. But what about generators, which could produce values *ad infinitum*?

Any time you use for to iterate over an iterable (basically, all sequence types and anything that defines __iter__() or __getitem__()), it needs to know when to stop iterating. Take a look at the code below:

```py
#!py
words = ['exceptions', 'are', 'useful']
for word in words:
    print(word)
```

How does for know when it's reached the last element in words and should stop trying to get more items? The answer may surprise you: the list raises a StopIteration exception.

In fact, all iterables follow this pattern. When a for statement is first evaluated, it calls iter() on the object being iterated over. This creates an iterator for the object, capable of returning the contents of the object in sequence. For the call to iter() to succeed, the object must either support the iteration protocol (by defining __iter__()) or the sequence protocol (by defining __getitem__()).

As it happens, both the __iter__() and __getitem__() functions are required to raise an exception when the items to iterate over are exhausted. __iter__() raises the StopIteration exception, as discussed earlier, and __getitem__() raises the IndexError exception. This is how for knows when to stop.

So whenever you're wondering if it's OK to use exceptions in Python, just remember this: for all but the most trivial programs, you're probably using them already.

1.4.2 Use Exceptions to Write Code in an ``EAFP'' Style

Code that doesn't use exceptions is always checking if it's OK to do something. In the harmful code below, the function `print_first_row` seems meek and overly-cautious. One can imagine it saying, ``I want to print the first result of a database query. Do I have a valid database connection? Did my query complete successfully? Are there any results?''

Code written in this manner must ask a number of different questions before it is convinced it's OK to do something. More importantly, once all questions have been answered to its satisfaction, *the code assumes whatever it is about to do will succeed*.

The `if` statements littered throughout the function give both the programmer and readers of the code a false sense of security. The programmer has checked everything she can think of that would prevent her code from working, so clearly nothing can go wrong, right? Someone reading the code would similarly assume that, with all those `if` statements, the function must handle all possible error conditions. Calling it shouldn't require any error handling.

Code written in this style is said to be written in a ``Look Before You Leap (LBYL)'' style. Every (thought of) pre-condition is explicitly checked. There's an obvious problem with this approach: if the code doesn't ask all of the right questions, bad things happen. It's rarely possible to anticipate everything that could go wrong. What's more, as the Python documentation astutely points out, code written in this style can fail badly in a multi-threaded environment. A condition that was true in an `if` statement may be false by the next line.

Alternatively, code written according to the principle, ``[It's] Easier to Ask for Forgiveness than Permission (EAFP),'' assumes things will go well and catches exceptions if they don't. It puts the code's true purpose front-and-center, increasing clarity. Rather than seeing a string of `if` statements and needing to remember what each checked before you even know what the code *wants* to do, EAFP-style code presents the end goal first. The error handling code that follows is easier to read; you already know the operation that could have failed.

1.4.2.1 Harmful

```python
def get_log_level(config_dict):
    if 'ENABLE_LOGGING' in config_dict:
        if config_dict['ENABLE_LOGGING'] != True:
            return None
        elif not 'DEFAULT_LOG_LEVEL' in config_dict:
            return None
        else: return config_dict['DEFAULT_LOG_LEVEL']
    else:
        return None
```

1.4.2.2 Idiomatic

```python
def get_log_level(config_dict):
    try:
        if config_dict['ENABLE_LOGGING']:
            return config_dict['DEFAULT_LOG_LEVEL']
    except KeyError:
        # if either value wasn't present, a
        # KeyError will be raised, so
        # return None
        return None
```

1.4.3 Avoid ``Swallowing" Useful Exceptions With Bare Except Clauses

A common mistake made by novices when using `exceptions` is to feel compelled to catch *any* `exception` code could raise. This is especially common when writing code using third-party packages; programmers encapsulate all uses of the package in `try` blocks followed by an `except` clause that doesn't specify an exception (also known as a ``bare" except clause). A generic error message like, ``something went wrong" may also be printed.

Exceptions have tracebacks and messages for a reason: to aid in debugging when something goes wrong. If you ``swallow" an exception with a bare `except` clause, you suppress genuinely useful debugging information. If you need to know whenever an exception occurs but don't intend to deal with it (say for logging purposes), add a bare `raise` to the end of your `except` block. The bare `raise` re-raises the exception that was caught. This way, your code runs and the user still gets useful information when something goes wrong.

Of course, there are valid reasons one would need to ensure some block of code *never* generates an exception. Almost none of the idioms described in this book are meant to be mechanically followed: use your head.

1.4.3.1 Harmful

```python
import requests
def get_json_response(url):
    try:
        r = requests.get(url)
        return r.json()
    except:
        print('Oops, something went wrong!')
        return None
```

1.4.3.2 Idiomatic

```python
import requests
def get_json_response(url):
    return requests.get(url).json()


# If we need to make note of the exception, we
# would write the function this way...
def alternate_get_json_response(url):
    try:
        r = requests.get(url)
        return r.json()
    except:
```

```
# do some logging here, but don't handle the exception
# ...
raise
```

Chapter 2

Working with Data

2.1 Variables

2.1.1 Avoid using a temporary variable when performing a **swap** of two values

There is no reason to swap using a temporary variable in Python. We can use tuples to make our intention more clear.

2.1.1.1 Harmful

```python
foo = 'Foo'
bar = 'Bar'
temp = foo
foo = bar
bar = temp
```

2.1.1.2 Idiomatic

```python
foo = 'Foo'
bar = 'Bar'
(foo, bar) = (bar, foo)
```

2.2   Strings

2.2.1   Chain `string` functions to make a simple series of transformations more clear

When applying a simple sequence of transformations on some datum, *chaining* the calls in a single expression is often more clear than creating a temporary variable for each step of the transformation. Too much chaining, however, can make your code harder to follow. ``No more than three chained functions'' is a good rule of thumb.

2.2.1.1   Harmful

```
book_info = ' The Three Musketeers: Alexandre Dumas'
formatted_book_info = book_info.strip()
formatted_book_info = formatted_book_info.upper()
formatted_book_info = formatted_book_info.replace(':', ' by')
```

2.2.1.2   Idiomatic

```
book_info = ' The Three Musketeers: Alexandre Dumas'
formatted_book_info = book_info.strip().upper().replace(':', ' by')
```

2.2.2 Use `''.join` when creating a single `string` for `list` elements

It's faster, uses less memory, and you'll see it everywhere anyway. Note that the two quotes represent the delimiter between `list` elements in the `string` we're creating. `''` just means we wish to concatenate the elements with no characters between them.

2.2.2.1 Harmful

```python
result_list = ['True', 'False', 'File not found']
result_string = ''
for result in result_list:
    result_string += result
```

2.2.2.2 Idiomatic

```python
result_list = ['True', 'False', 'File not found']
result_string = ''.join(result_list)
```

2.2.3 Prefer the `format` function for formatting strings

There are three general ways of formatting strings (that is, creating a `string` that is a mix of hard-coded strings and `string` variables). Easily the worst approach is to use the + operator to concatenate a mix of static strings and variables. Using ``old-style'' string formatting is slightly better. It makes use of a format string and the % operator to fill in values, much like `printf` does in other languages.

The clearest and most idiomatic way to format strings is to use the `format` function. Like old-style formatting, it takes a format string and replaces placeholders with values. The similarities end there, though. With the `format` function, we can use named placeholders, access their attributes, and control padding and string width, among a number of other things. The `format` function makes string formatting clean and concise.

2.2.3.1 Harmful

```python
def get_formatted_user_info_worst(user):
    # Tedious to type and prone to conversion errors
    return 'Name: ' + user.name + ', Age: ' + \
            str(user.age) + ', Sex: ' + user.sex


def get_formatted_user_info_slightly_better(user):
    # No visible connection between the format string placeholders
    # and values to use. Also, why do I have to know the type?
    # Don't these types all have __str__ functions?
    return 'Name: %s, Age: %i, Sex: %c' % (
        user.name, user.age, user.sex)
```

2.2.3.2 Idiomatic

```python
def get_formatted_user_info(user):
    # Clear and concise. At a glance I can tell exactly what
    # the output should be. Note: this string could be returned
    # directly, but the string itself is too long to fit on the
    # page.
    output = 'Name: {user.name}, Age: {user.age}, Sex: {user.sex}'.format(user=user)
    return output
```

2.3 Lists

2.3.1 Use a `list comprehension` to create a transformed version of an existing list

`list comprehensions`, when used judiciously, increase clarity in code that builds a list from existing data. This is especially true when elements are both checked for some condition *and* transformed in some way.

There are also (usually) performance benefits to using a `list comprehension` (or alternately, a `generator expression`) due to optimizations in the cPython interpreter.

2.3.1.1 Harmful

```python
some_other_list = range(10)
some_list = list()
for element in some_other_list:
    if is_prime(element):
        some_list.append(element + 5)
```

2.3.1.2 Idiomatic

```python
some_other_list = range(10)
some_list = [element + 5
             for element in some_other_list
             if is_prime(element)]
```

2.3.2   Prefer **xrange** to **range** unless you need the resulting list

Both xrange and range let you iterate over a list of numbers in a specified range. xrange, however, doesn't store the entire list in memory. Much of the time this isn't an issue. If you're working with very large number ranges (or breaking out of a loop over a very large range), the memory and performance gains can be substantial.

2.3.2.1   Harmful

```python
# A loop over a large range that breaks out
# early: a double whammy!
even_number = int()
for index in range (1000000):
    if index % 2 == 0:
        even_number = index
        break
```

2.3.2.2   Idiomatic

```python
even_number = int()
for index in xrange(1000000):
    if index % 2 == 0:
        even_number = index
        break
```

2.4 Dictionaries

2.4.1 Use a `dict` as a substitute for a `switch...case` statement

Unlike many other languages, Python doesn't have a `switch...case` construct. Typically, `switch` inspects the value of an expression and jumps to the `case` statement with the given value. It's a shortcut for calling a single piece of code out of a number of possibilities based on a runtime value. For example, if we're writing a command-line based calculator, a switch statement may be used on the operator typed by the user. ``+" would call the `addition()` function, ``*" the `multiplication()` function, and so on.

The naive alternative in Python is to write a series of `if...else` statements. This gets old quickly. Thankfully, functions are first-class objects in Python, so we can treat them the same as any other variable. *This is a very powerful concept*, and many other powerful concepts use first-class functions as a building block.

So how does this help us with `switch...case` statements? Rather than trying to emulate the exact functionality, we can take advantage of the fact that functions are first-class object and can be stored as values in a `dict`. Returning to the calculator example, storing the string operator (e.g. ``+") as the key and it's associated function as the value, we arrive at a clear, readable way to achieve the same functionality as `switch...case`.

This idiom is useful for more than just picking a function to dispatch using a string key. It can be generalized to *anything* that can be used as a `dict` key, which in Python is just about everything. Using this method, one could create a Factory class that chooses which type to instantiate via a parameter. Or it could be used to store states and their transitions when building a state machine. Once you fully appreciate the power of ``everything is an object", you'll find elegant solutions to once-difficult problems.

2.4.1.1 Harmful

```python
def apply_operation(left_operand, right_operand, operator):
    if operator == '+':
        return left_operand + right_operand
    elif operator == '-':
        return left_operand - right_operand
    elif operator == '*':
        return left_operand * right_operand
    elif operator == '/':
        return left_operand / right_operand
```

2.4.1.2 Idiomatic

```python
def apply_operation(left_operand, right_operand, operator):
    import operator as op
```

```python
operator_mapper = {'+': op.add, '-': op.sub,
        '*': op.mul, '/': op.truediv}
return operator_mapper[operator](left_operand, right_operand)
```

2.4.2 Use the `default` parameter of `dict.get` to provide default values

Often overlooked in the definition of `dict.get` is the `default` parameter. Without using `default` (or the `collections.default` class), your code will be littered with confusing `if` statements. Remember, strive for clarity.

2.4.2.1 Harmful

```python
log_severity = None
if 'severity' in configuration:
    log_severity = configuration['severity']
else:
    log_severity = 'Info'
```

2.4.2.2 Idiomatic

```python
log_severity = configuration.get('severity', 'Info')
```

2.4.3 Use a `dict comprehension` to build a `dict` clearly and efficiently

The `list comprehension` is a well-known Python construct. Less well known is the `dict comprehension`. Its purpose is identical: to construct a `dict` in place using the widely understood `comprehension` syntax.

2.4.3.1 Harmful

```python
user_email = {}
for user in users_list:
    if user.email:
        user_email[user.name] = user.email
```

2.4.3.2 Idiomatic

```python
user_email = {user.name: user.email
              for user in users_list if user.email}
```

2.5 Sets

2.5.1 Understand and use the mathematical `set` operations

`sets` are an easy to understand data structure. Like a `dict` with keys but no values, the `set` class implements the `Iterable` and `Container` interfaces. Thus, a `set` can be used in a `for` loop or as the subject of an `in` statement.

For programmers who haven't seen a Set data type before, it may appear to be of limited use. Key to understanding their usefulness is understanding their origin in mathematics. Set Theory is the branch of mathematics devoted to the study of sets. Understanding the basic mathematical set operations is the key to harnessing their power.

Don't worry; you don't need a degree in math to understand or use sets. You just need to remember a few simple operations:

Union The set of elements in A, B, or both A and B (written A | B in Python).

Intersection The set of elements in both A and B (written A & B in Python).

Difference The set of elements in A but not B (written A - B in Python).
    *Note: order matters here. A - B is not necessarily the same as B - A.

Symmetric Difference The set of elements in either A or B, but not both A *and* B (written A ^ B in Python).

When working with lists of data, a common task is finding the elements that appear in all of the lists. Any time you need to choose elements from two or more sequences based on properties of sequence membership, **look to use a set**.

Below, we'll explore some typical examples.

2.5.1.1 Harmful

```python
def get_both_popular_and_active_users():
    # Assume the following two functions each return a
    # list of user names
    most_popular_users = get_list_of_most_popular_users()
    most_active_users = get_list_of_most_active_users()
    popular_and_active_users = []
    for user in most_active_users:
        if user in most_popular_users:
            popular_and_active_users.append(user)

    return popular_and_active_users
```

2.5.1.2 Idiomatic

```python
def get_both_popular_and_active_users():
    # Assume the following two functions each return a
    # list of user names
    return(set(
        get_list_of_most_active_users()) & set(
            get_list_of_most_popular_users()))
```

2.5.2 Use a `set comprehension` to generate sets concisely

The `set comprehension` syntax is relatively new in Python and, therefore, often overlooked. Just as a `list` can be generated using a `list comprehension`, a `set` can be generated using a `set comprehension`. In fact, the syntax is nearly identical (modulo the enclosing characters).

2.5.2.1 Harmful

```python
users_first_names = set()
for user in users:
    users_first_names.add(user.first_name)
```

2.5.2.2 Idiomatic

```python
users_first_names = {user.first_name for user in users}
```

2.5.3   Use sets to eliminate duplicate entries from `Iterable` containers

It's quite common to have a `list` or `dict` with duplicate values. In a `list` of all surnames of employees at a large company, we're bound to encounter common surnames more than once in the list. If we need a list of all the *unique* surnames, we can use a `set` to do the work for us. Three aspects of `sets` make them the perfect answer to our problem:

1. A `set` contains only unique elements
2. Adding an already existing element to a `set` is essentially ``ignored"
3. A `set` can be built from any `Iterable` whose elements are hashable

Continuing the example, we may have an existing `display` function that accepts a `sequence` and displays its elements in one of many formats. After creating a `set` from our original `list`, will we need to change our `display` function?

Nope. Assuming our `display` function is implemented reasonably, our `set` can be used as a drop-in replacement for a `list`. This works thanks to the fact that a `set`, like a `list`, is an `Iterable` and can thus be used in a `for` loop, `list` `comprehension`, etc.

2.5.3.1   Harmful

```python
unique_surnames = []
for surname in employee_surnames:
    if surname not in unique_surnames:
        unique_surnames.append(surname)


def display(elements, output_format='html'):
    if output_format == 'std_out':
        for element in elements:
            print(element)
    elif output_format == 'html':
        as_html = '<ul>'
        for element in elements:
            as_html += '<li>{}</li>'.format(element)
        return as_html + '</ul>'
    else:
        raise RuntimeError('Unknown format {}'.format(output_format))
```

2.5.3.2   Idiomatic

```python
unique_surnames = set(employee_surnames)

def display(elements, output_format='html'):
    if output_format == 'std_out':
        for element in elements:
            print(element)
    elif output_format == 'html':
        as_html = '<ul>'
        for element in elements:
            as_html += '<li>{}</li>'.format(element)
        return as_html + '</ul>'
    else:
        raise RuntimeError('Unknown format {}'.format(output_format))
```

2.6 Tuples

2.6.1 Use `collections.namedtuple` to make **tuple**-heavy code more clear

The `tuple` is a fantastically useful data structure in Python. Many libraries use `tuples` to represent data which is logically arranged in a spreadsheet-like structure. Most database libraries, for example, use `tuples` to represent a single row in a database table. Queries that return multiple rows are represented as lists of `tuples`.

When working with `tuples` in this way, each index in the `tuple` has a specific meaning. In our database example (where a `tuple` represents a single result row) each index corresponds to a specific column. Writing code that forces you to remember which index corresponds to which column (i.e. `result[3]` is the `salary` column) is confusing and error prone.

Luckily, the `collections` module has an elegant solution: `collections.namedtuple`. A namedtuple is a normal `tuple` with a few extra capabilities. Most importantly, `namedtuples` give you the ability to access fields by names rather than by index.

`collections.namedtuple` is a powerful tool for increasing the readability and maintainability of code. The example above was but one of the *many* cases where `collections.namedtuple` is useful.

2.6.1.1 Harmful

```python
# Assume the 'employees' table has the following columns:
# first_name, last_name, department, manager, salary, hire_date
def print_employee_information(db_connection):
    db_cursor = db_connection.cursor()
    results = db_cursor.execute('select * from employees').fetchall()
    for row in results:
        # It's basically impossible to follow what's getting printed
        print(row[1] + ', ' + row[0] + ' was hired '
        'on ' + row[5] + ' (for $' + row[4] + ' per annum)'
        ' into the ' + row[2] + ' department and reports to ' + row[3])
```

2.6.1.2 Idiomatic

```python
# Assume the 'employees' table has the following columns:
# first_name, last_name, department, manager, salary, hire_date
from collections import namedtuple
```

```
EmployeeRow = namedtuple('EmployeeRow', ['first_name',
'last_name', 'department', 'manager', 'salary', 'hire_date'])

EMPLOYEE_INFO_STRING = '{last}, {first} was hired on {date} \
 ${salary} per annum) into the {department} department and reports to \
ager}'

def print_employee_information(db_connection):
    db_cursor = db_connection.cursor()
    results = db_cursor.execute('select * from employees').fetchall()
    for row in results:
        employee = EmployeeRow._make(row)

        # It's now almost impossible to print a field in the wrong place
        print(EMPLOYEE_INFO_STRING.format(
            last=employee.last_name,
            first=employee.first_name,
            date=employee.hire_date,
            salary=employee.salary,
            department=employee.department,
            manager=employee.manager))
```

2.6.2   Use _ as a placeholder for data in a tuple that should be ignored

When setting a `tuple` equal to some ordered data, oftentimes not all of the data is actually needed. Instead of creating throwaway variables with confusing names, use the _ as a placeholder to tell the reader, ``This data will be discarded.''

2.6.2.1   Harmful

```python
(name, age, temp, temp2) = get_user_info(user)
if age > 21:
    output = '{name} can drink!'.format(name=name)
# "Wait, where are temp and temp2 being used?"
```

2.6.2.2   Idiomatic

```python
(name, age, _, _) = get_user_info(user)
if age > 21:
    output = '{name} can drink!'.format(name=name)
# "Clearly, only name and age are interesting"
```

2.6.3 Use `tuples` to unpack data

In Python, it is possible to ``unpack" data for multiple assignment. Those familiar with LISP may know this as `destructuring bind`.

2.6.3.1 Harmful

```python
list_from_comma_separated_value_file = ['dog', 'Fido', 10]
animal = list_from_comma_separated_value_file[0]
name = list_from_comma_separated_value_file[1]
age = list_from_comma_separated_value_file[2]
output = ('{name} the {animal} is {age} years old'.format(
    animal=animal, name=name, age=age))
```

2.6.3.2 Idiomatic

```python
list_from_comma_separated_value_file = ['dog', 'Fido', 10]
(animal, name, age) = list_from_comma_separated_value_file
output = ('{name} the {animal} is {age} years old'.format(
    animal=animal, name=name, age=age))
```

2.6.4 Use a `tuple` to return multiple values from a function

Oftentimes, it's necessary or desirable to return multiple values from a single function. I've seen a good amount of Python code written by novices that twists itself into knots trying to get around the incorrect assumption that a function can only return one logical value. While it's true that only one *object* can be returned from a function, that object may contain multiple logical values. A `tuple` is ideally suited to be used as a way to return multiple values from a function.

This is one of those patterns you'll see all the time when reading Python code in the standard library or third-party packages. It's also an idiom that sounds obvious when you hear or see it, but is not something those new to the language typically divine on their own.

2.6.4.1 Harmful

```python
from collections import Counter

STATS_FORMAT = """Statistics:
Mean: {mean}
Median: {median}
Mode: {mode}"""

def calculate_mean(value_list):
    return float(sum(value_list) / len(value_list))

def calculate_median(value_list):
    return value_list[int(len(value_list) / 2)]

def calculate_mode(value_list):
    return Counter(value_list).most_common(1)[0][0]

values = [10, 20, 20, 30]
mean = calculate_mean(values)
median = calculate_median(values)
mode = calculate_mode(values)

print(STATS_FORMAT.format(mean=mean, median=median,
        mode=mode))
```

2.6.4.2 Idiomatic

```python
from collections import Counter

STATS_FORMAT = """Statistics:
Mean: {mean}
Median: {median}
Mode: {mode}"""

def calculate_staistics(value_list):
    mean = float(sum(value_list) / len(value_list))
    median = value_list[int(len(value_list) / 2)]
    mode = Counter(value_list).most_common(1)[0][0]
    return (mean, median, mode)

(mean, median, mode) = calculate_staistics([10, 20, 20, 30])
print(STATS_FORMAT.format(mean=mean, median=median, mode=mode))
```

2.7 Classes

2.7.1 Use leading underscores in function and variable names to denote ``private'' data

All attributes of a class, be they data or functions, are inherently ``public'' in Python. A client is free to add attributes to a class after it's been defined. In addition, if the class is meant to be inherited from, a subclass may unwittingly change an attribute of the base class. Lastly, it's generally useful to be able to signal to users of your class that certain portions are logically public (and won't be changed in a backwards incompatible way) while other attributes are purely internal implementation artifacts and shouldn't be used directly by client code using the class.

A number of widely followed conventions have arisen to make the author's intention more explicit and help avoid unintentional naming conflicts. While the following two idioms are commonly referred to as `nothing more than conventions,' both of them, in fact, alter the behavior of the interpreter when used.

First, attributes to be `protected', which are not meant to be used directly by clients, should be prefixed with a single underscore. Second, `private' attributes not meant to be accessible by a subclass should be prefixed by *two underscores*. Of course, these are (mostly) merely conventions. Nothing would stop a client from being able to access your `private' attributes, but the convention is so widely used you likely won't run into developers that purposely choose not to honor it. It's just another example of the Python community settling on a single way of accomplishing something.

Before, I hinted that the single and double underscore prefix were more than mere conventions. Few developers are aware of the fact that prepending attribute names in a class *does actually do something*. Prepending a single underscore means that the symbol won't be imported if the `**all**' idiom is used. Prepending two underscores to an attribute name invokes Python's name mangling. This has the effect of making it far less likely someone who subclasses your class with inadvertently replace your class's attribute with something unintended. If Foo is a class, the definition def __bar() will be `mangled' to _classname__attributename.

2.7.1.1 Harmful

```python
class Foo(object):
    def __init__(self):
        self.id = 8
        self.value = self.get_value()

    def get_value(self):
        pass

    def should_destroy_earth(self):
        return self.id == 42
```

```python
class Baz(Foo):
    def get_value(self, some_new_parameter):
        """Since 'get_value' is called from the base class's
        __init__ method and the base class definition doesn't
        take a parameter, trying to create a Baz instance will
        fail

        """
        pass

class Qux(Foo):
    """We aren't aware of Foo's internals, and we innocently
    create an instance attribute named 'id' and set it to 42.
    This overwrites Foo's id attribute and we inadvertently
    blow up the earth.

    """

    def __init__(self):
        super(Qux, self).__init__()
        self.id = 42
        # No relation to Foo's id, purely coincidental

q = Qux()
b = Baz()  # Raises 'TypeError'
q.should_destroy_earth()  # returns True
q.id == 42  # returns True
```

2.7.1.2 Idiomatic

```python
class Foo(object):
    def __init__(self):
        """Since 'id' is of vital importance to us, we don't
        want a derived class accidentally overwriting it. We'll
        prepend with double underscores to introduce name
        mangling.
        """
        self.__id = 8
```

```python
        self.value = self.__get_value() # Call our 'private copy'

    def get_value(self):
        pass

    def should_destroy_earth(self):
        return self.__id == 42

    # Here, we're storing a 'private copy' of get_value,
    # and assigning it to '__get_value'. Even if a derived
    # class overrides get_value in a way incompatible with
    # ours, we're fine
    __get_value = get_value



class Baz(Foo):
    def get_value(self, some_new_parameter):
        pass

class Qux(Foo):
    def __init__(self):
        """Now when we set 'id' to 42, it's not the same 'id'
        that 'should_destroy_earth' is concerned with. In fact,
        if you inspect a Qux object, you'll find it doesn't
        have an __id attribute. So we can't mistakenly change
        Foo's __id attribute even if we wanted to.

        """
        self.id = 42
        # No relation to Foo's id, purely coincidental
        super(Qux, self).__init__()

q = Qux()
b = Baz()   # Works fine now
q.should_destroy_earth()  # returns False
q.id == 42   # returns True
```

2.7.2   Use `properties` to ``future-proof'' your class implementation

Oftentimes, it is convenient to provide direct access to a class's data attributes. A `Point` class, for example, may have x and y attributes rather than using ``getter'' and ``setter'' functions. However, there's a reason ``getters'' and ``setters'' exist (in addition to further frustrating Java programmers): you never know when what once was pure data will require calculation instead. Suppose we have a `Product` class that is initizialized with a product's name and its price, both of which we simply set as attributes of the class. If we are later asked to apply tax to a product's price automatically, does that mean we go through the code and change all occurrences of `product.price` to `product.price * TAX_RATE`? Not if we thought ahead and made `price` a property!

2.7.2.1   Harmful

```python
class Product(object):
    def __init__(self, name, price):
        self.name = name
        # We could try to apply the tax rate here, but the object's price
        # may be modified later, which erases the tax
        self.price = price
```

2.7.2.2   Idiomatic

```python
class Product(object):
    def __init__(self, name, price):
        self.name = name
        self._price = price

    @property
    def price(self):
        # now if we need to change how price is calculated, we can do it
        # here (or in the "setter" and __init__)
        return self._price * TAX_RATE

    @price.setter
    def price(self, value):
        # The "setter" function must have the same name as the property
        self._price = value
```

2.7.3 Define `__str__` in a class to show a human-readable representation

When defining a class that is likely to be used with `print()`, the default Python representation isn't too helpful. By defining a `__str__` method, you can control how calling `print` on an instance of your class will look.

2.7.3.1 Harmful

```python
class Point(object):
    def __init__(self, x, y):
        self.x = x
        self.y = y

p = Point(1, 2)
print (p)

# Prints '<__main__.Point object at 0x91ebd0>'
```

2.7.3.2 Idiomatic

```python
class Point(object):
    def __init__(self, x, y):
        self.x = x
        self.y = y

    def __str__(self):
        return '{0}, {1}'.format(self.x, self.y)

p = Point(1, 2)
print (p)

# Prints '1, 2'
```

2.8 Context Managers

2.8.1 Use a `context manager` to ensure resources are properly managed

Similar to the *RAII* principle in languages like C++ and D, `context managers` (objects meant to be used with the `with` statement) can make resource management both safer and more explicit. The canonical example is file IO.

Take a look at the ``Harmful'' code below. What happens if `raise_exception` does, in fact, raise an exception? Since we haven't caught it in the code below, it will propagate up the stack. We've hit an exit point in our code that might have been overlooked, and we now have no way to close the opened file.

There are a number of classes in the standard library that support or use a `context manager`. In addition, user defined classes can be easily made to work with a `context manager` by defining `__enter__` and `__exit__` methods. Functions may be wrapped with `context managers` through the `contextlib` module.

2.8.1.1 Harmful

```python
file_handle = open(path_to_file, 'r')
for line in file_handle.readlines():
    if raise_exception(line):
        print('No! An Exception!')
```

2.8.1.2 Idiomatic

```python
with open(path_to_file, 'r') as file_handle:
    for line in file_handle:
        if raise_exception(line):
            print('No! An Exception!')
```

2.9 Generators

2.9.1 Prefer a **generator expression** to a **list comprehension** for simple iteration

When dealing with a sequence, it is common to need to iterate over a slightly modified version of the sequence a single time. For example, you may want to print out the first names of all of your users in all capital letters.

Your first instinct should be to build and iterate over the sequence in place. A list comprehension seems ideal, but there's an even better Python built-in: a generator expression.

The main difference? A list comprehension generates a list object and fills in all of the elements immediately. For large lists, this can be prohibitively expensive. The generator returned by a generator expression, on the other hand, generates each element ``on-demand''. That list of uppercase user names you want to print out? Probably not a problem. But what if you wanted to write out the title of every book known to the Library of Congress? You'd likely run out of memory in generating your list comprehension, while a generator expression won't bat an eyelash. A logical extension of the way generator expressions work is that you can use a them on infinite sequences.

2.9.1.1 Harmful

```
for uppercase_name in [name.upper() for name in get_all_usernames()]:
    process_normalized_username(uppercase_name)
```

2.9.1.2 Idiomatic

```
for uppercase_name in (name.upper() for name in get_all_usernames()):
    process_normalized_username(uppercase_name)
```

2.9.2 Use a `generator` to lazily load infinite sequences

Often, it's useful to provide a way to iterate over a `sequence` that's essentially infinite. Other times, you need to provide an interface to a `sequence` that's incredibly expensive to calculate, and you don't want your user sitting on their hands waiting for you to finish building a list.

In both cases, `generators` are your friend. A generator is a special type of coroutine which returns an `iterable`. The state of the `generator` is saved, so that the next call into the `generator` continues where it left off. In the examples below, we'll see how to use a `generator` to help in each of the cases mentioned above.

2.9.2.1 Harmful

```python
def get_twitter_stream_for_keyword(keyword):
    """Get's the 'live stream', but only at the moment
    the function is initially called. To get more entries,
    the client code needs to keep calling
    'get_twitter_livestream_for_user'. Not ideal.
    """

    imaginary_twitter_api = ImaginaryTwitterAPI()
    if imaginary_twitter_api.can_get_stream_data(keyword):
        return imaginary_twitter_api.get_stream(keyword)

current_stream = get_twitter_stream_for_keyword('#jeffknupp')
for tweet in current_stream:
    process_tweet(tweet)

# Uh, I want to keep showing tweets until the program is quit.
# What do I do now? Just keep calling
# get_twitter_stream_for_keyword?  That seems stupid.

def get_list_of_incredibly_complex_calculation_results(data):
    return [first_incredibly_long_calculation(data),
            second_incredibly_long_calculation(data),
            third_incredibly_long_calculation(data),
            ]
```

2.9.2.2 Idiomatic

```python
def get_twitter_stream_for_keyword(keyword):
    """Now, 'get_twitter_stream_for_keyword' is a generator
    and will continue to generate Iterable pieces of data
    one at a time until 'can_get_stream_data(user)' is
    False (which may be never).

    """

    imaginary_twitter_api = ImaginaryTwitterAPI()
    while imaginary_twitter_api.can_get_stream_data(keyword):
        yield imaginary_twitter_api.get_stream(keyword)

# Because it's a generator, I can sit in this loop until
# the client wants to break out
for tweet in get_twitter_stream_for_keyword('#jeffknupp'):
    if got_stop_signal:
        break
    process_tweet(tweet)

def get_list_of_incredibly_complex_calculation_results(data):
    """A simple example to be sure, but now when the client
    code iterates over the call to
    'get_list_of_incredibly_complex_calculation_results',
    we only do as much work as necessary to generate the
    current item.

    """
    yield first_incredibly_long_calculation(data)
    yield second_incredibly_long_calculation(data)
    yield third_incredibly_long_calculation(data)
```

Chapter 3

Organizing Your Code

3.1 Formatting

3.1.1 Use all capital letters when declaring global constant values

To distinguish `constants` defined at the module level (or global in a single script) from imported names, use all uppercase letters.

3.1.1.1 Harmful

```python
seconds_in_a_day = 60 * 60 * 24
# ...
def display_uptime(uptime_in_seconds):
    percentage_run_time = (
        uptime_in_seconds/seconds_in_a_day) * 100
    # "Huh!? Where did seconds_in_a_day come from?"

    return 'The process was up {percent} percent of the day'.format(
        percent=int(percentage_run_time))
# ...
uptime_in_seconds = 60 * 60 * 24
display_uptime(uptime_in_seconds)
```

3.1.1.2 Idiomatic

```python
SECONDS_IN_A_DAY = 60 * 60 * 24
# ...
def display_uptime(uptime_in_seconds):
    percentage_run_time = (
        uptime_in_seconds/SECONDS_IN_A_DAY) * 100
    # "Clearly SECONDS_IN_A_DAY is a constant defined
    # elsewhere in this module."

    return 'The process was up {percent} percent of the day'.format(
        percent=int(percentage_run_time))


# ...
uptime_in_seconds = 60 * 60 * 24
display_uptime(uptime_in_seconds)
```

3.1.2   Format your code according to PEP8

Python has a language-defined standard set of formatting rules known as PEP8. If you're browsing commit messages on Python projects, you'll likely find them littered with references to PEP8 cleanup. The reason is simple: if we all agree on a common set of naming and formatting conventions, Python code as a whole becomes instantly more accessible to both novice and experienced developers. PEP8 is perhaps the most explicit example of idioms within the Python community. Read the PEP, install a PEP8 style-checking plugin for your editor (they all have one), and start writing your code in a way that other Python developers will appreciate. Listed below are a few examples.

Identifier Type	Format	Example
Class	Camel case	class StringManipulator():
Variable	Words joined by _	joined_by_underscore = True
Function	Words joined by _	def multi_word_name(words):
Constant	All uppercase	SECRET_KEY = 42

Table 3.1: *Unless wildly unreasonable, abbreviations should not be used (acronyms are fine if in common use, like `HTTP')*

Basically everything not listed should follow the variable/function naming conventions of `Words joined by an underscore'.

3.1.3 Avoid placing multiple statements on a single line

Though the language definition allows one to use ; to delineate statements, doing so without reason makes one's code harder to read. When multiple statements occur on the same line as an if, else, or elif, the situation is even further confused.

3.1.3.1 Harmful

```python
for element in my_list: print (element); print ('--------')
```

3.1.3.2 Idiomatic

```python
for element in my_list:
    print(element)
    print('--------')
```

3.2 Documentation

3.2.1 Follow the `docstring` conventions described in PEP-257

Given that Python has an official stance on code formatting, it should come as no surprise that a similar set of recommendations exist for documentation. In particular, PEP-257 sets forth rules for writing and formatting a `docstring`. A `docstring` is (according to PEP-257), ``a string literal that occurs as the first statement in a module, function, class, or method definition." Basically, it's a line or set of lines enclosed in triple-quotes which immediately follow `def`, `class`, or reside at the top of a file.

Writing a ``good" `docstring`, like writing good documentation in general, takes practice. Following the rules in PEP-257 will help a good deal. Two in particular will get you 90% of the way there: Everything public or exported should have a `docstring`, and how to properly format them.

Writing documentation for all of a class's public methods and everything exported by a module (including the module itself) may seem like overkill, but there's a very good reason to do it: helping documentation tools. Third-party software like Sphinx are able to automatically generate documentation (in formats like HTML, LaTex, man pages, etc) from properly documented code. If you decide to use such a tool, all of your classes' public methods and all exported functions in a module will automatically have entries in the generated documentation. If you've only written documentation for half of these, the documentation is far less useful to an end user. Imagine trying to read the official Python documentation for `itertools` if half of the functions listed only their signature and nothing more.

In addition, this is one of those rules that helps remove a cognitive burden on the programmer. By following this rule, you never have to ask yourself ``does this function merit a docstring?" or try to determine the threshold for documentation. Just follow the rule and don't worry about it. Of course, use common sense if there's a good reason *not* to write documentation for something.

The formatting rules help both documentation tools and IDEs. Using a predictable structure to your documentation allows it to be parsed in a useful way. For example, the first line of a `docstring` should be a one-sentence summary. If more lines are necessary, they are separated from the first line by a blank line. This allows documentation tools and IDEs to present a summary of the code in question and hide more detailed documentation if it's not needed. There's really no good reason not to follow the formatting rules (that I can think of), and you're only helping yourself by doing so.

3.2.1.1 Harmful

```python
def calculate_statistics(value_list):

    # calculates various statistics for a list of numbers

    <The body of the function>
```

3.2.1.2   Idiomatic

```python
def calculate_statistics(value_list):
    """Return a tuple containing the  mean, median,
    and mode of a list of integers


    Arguments:
    value_list -- a list of integer values

    """
    <The body of the function>
```

3.2.2 Use Inline Documentation Sparingly

Novice programmers, if they document at all, tend to *over* document their code. Writing an appropriate `docstring` is one thing, but writing inline comments about almost every line of code is quite another. Too much documentation is *more* of a burden on readers and maintainers than none at all. Your goal should be to write self-documenting code. Idiomatic Python is so clear that it reads as if it *were* documentation. If you frequently find the need to document a single line or small set of lines, it's an indication your code isn't as clear as it should be. Worse, if you come back and make changes in a month, you need to remember to change the documentation *and* the code. The only thing worse than too much documentation is **wrong** documentation.

3.2.2.1 Harmful

```python
def calculate_mean(numbers):
    """Return the mean of a list of numbers"""

    # If the list is empty, we have no mean!
    if not numbers:
        return 0

    # A variable to keep track of the running sum
    total = 0

    # Iterate over each number in the list
    for number in numbers:
        total += number

    # Divide the sum of all the numbers by how
    # many numbers were in the list
    # to arrive at the sum. Return this value.
    return total / len(numbers)
```

3.2.2.2 Idiomatic

```python
def calculate_mean(numbers):
    """Return the mean of a list of numbers"""
    return sum(numbers) / len(numbers)
```

3.2.3 Document *What* Something Does, Not How

When writing a docstring, be sure to document *what* the code does rather than *how* it does it. Readers of the documentation don't need to know how a function works to use it. Indeed, describing how a function works in its documentation creates a leaky abstraction. Further, it increases the probability that the code and documentation will diverge at some point. To see why, look at the harmful example below; changing the method for determining if a number is prime requires a corresponding change the function's docstring. If the docstring is not updated, the documentation now says one thing but the code says another. The idiomatic example requires no documentation changes when the underlying implementation changes.

3.2.3.1 Harmful

```python
def is_prime(number):
    """Mod all numbers from 2 -> number and return True
    if the value is never 0"""

    for candidate in range(2, number):
        if number % candidate == 0:
            print(candidate)
            print(number % candidate)
            return False

    return number > 0
```

3.2.3.2 Idiomatic

```python
def is_prime(number):
    """Return True if number is prime"""

    for candidate in range(2, number):
        if number % candidate == 0:
            return False

    return number > 0
```

3.3   Imports

3.3.1   Arrange your `import` statements in a standard order

As projects grow (especially those using web frameworks), so do the number of import statements. Stick *all* of your `import` statements at the top of each file, choose a standard order for your import statements, and stick with it. While the actual ordering is not as important, the following is the order recommended by Python's Programming FAQ:

1. standard library modules
2. third-party library modules installed in site-packages
3. modules local to the current project

Many choose to arrange the imports in (roughly) alphabetical order. Others think that's ridiculous. In reality, it doesn't matter. What matters it that you *do* choose a standard order (and follow it of course).

3.3.1.1   Harmful

```python
import os.path

# Some function and class definitions,
# one of which uses os.path
# ....

import concurrent.futures
from flask import render_template

# Stuff using futures and Flask's render_template
# ....

from flask import (Flask, request, session, g,
    redirect, url_for, abort,
    render_template, flash, _app_ctx_stack)
import requests

# Code using flask and requests
# ....

if __name__ == '__main__':
```

```python
# Imports when imported as a module are not so
# costly that they need to be relegated to inside
# an 'if __name__ == '__main__'' block...
import this_project.utilities.sentient_network as skynet
import this_project.widgets
import sys
```

3.3.1.2 Idiomatic

```python
# Easy to see exactly what my dependencies are and where to
# make changes if a module or package name changes
import concurrent.futures
import os.path
import sys
from flask import (Flask, request, session, g,
    redirect, url_for, abort,
    render_template, flash, _app_ctx_stack)
import requests
import this_project.utilities.sentient_network as skynet
import this_project.widgets
```

3.3.2 Prefer `absolute imports` to `relative imports`

When importing a module, you have two choices of the import ``style'' to use: `absolute imports` or `relative imports`. `absolute imports` specify a module's location (like `<package>.<module>.<submodule>`) from a location which is reachable from `sys.path`.

Relative imports specify a module relative to the current module's location on the file system. If you are the module `package.sub_package.module` and need to import `package.other_module`, you can do so using the dotted `relative import` syntax: `from ..other_module import foo`. A single `.` represents the current package a module is contained in (like in a file system). Each additional `.` is taken to mean ``the parent package of'', one level per dot. Note that `relative imports` must use the `from ... import ...` style. `import foo` is always treated as an absolute import.

Alternatively, using an `absolute import` you would write

`import package.other_module` (possibly with an `as` clause to alias the module to a shorter name.

Why, then, should you prefer absolute imports to relative? Relative imports clutter a module's namespace. By writing `from foo import bar`, you've bound the name `bar` in your module's namespace. To those reading your code, it will not be clear where `bar` came from, especially if used in a complicated function or large module. `foo.bar`, however, makes it perfectly clear where `bar` is defined. The Python programming FAQ goes so far as to say, ``Never use relative package imports.''

3.3.2.1 Harmful

```
# My location is package.sub_package.module
# and I want to import package.other_module.
# The following should be avoided:

from ...package import other_module
```

3.3.2.2 Idiomatic

```
# My location is package.sub_package.another_sub_package.module
# and I want to import package.other_module.
# Either of the following are acceptable:

import package.other_module
import package.other_module as other
```

3.3.3 Do not use `from foo import` * to import the contents of a module.

Considering the previous idiom, this one should be obvious. Using an asterisk in an import (as in `from foo import *`) is an easy way to clutter your namespace. This may even cause issues if there are clashes between names you define and those defined in the package.

But what if you have to import a number of names from the `foo` package? Simple. Make use of the fact that parenthesis can be used to group import statements. You won't have to write 10 lines of import statements from the same module, and your namespace remains (relatively) clean.

Better yet, simply use `absolute imports`. If the package/module name is too long, use an `as` clause to shorten it.

3.3.3.1 Harmful

```
from foo import *
```

3.3.3.2 Idiomatic

```
from foo import (bar, baz, qux,
        quux, quuux)

# or even better...
import foo
```

3.4   Modules and Packages

3.4.1   Make use of `__init.py__` files to simplify package interfaces

Much of the time, the most interaction we have with an `__init.py__` file is calling `touch __init__.py` to make a directory a package. That file, however, can contain useful code that controls how a package is initialized and what names are visible. If you have a package with dozens of modules, only one or two of which are meant to be used by client code, then `__init__.py` is your friend. You can import modules from all over your package and make them available via the **init** module. This lets client code refer to classes that may be nested 4 levels deep as if they were declared in the main module.

This is very commonly done in libraries and frameworks, like Flask, which aim to create simple interfaces for client code.

3.4.1.1   Harmful

```
# If the gizmo directory has an emtpy __init__.py,
# imports like the ones below are necessary, even
# if Gizmo and GizmoHelper are all that clients should ever need to use
from gizmo.client.interface import Gizmo
from gizmo.client.contrib.utils import GizmoHelper
```

3.4.1.2   Idiomatic

```
# __init__.py:

from gizmo.client.interface import Gizmo
from gizmo.client.contrib.utils import GizmoHelper

#client code:
from gizmo import Gizmo, GizmoHelper
```

3.4.2   Use `modules` for encapsulation where other languages would use Objects

While Python certainly supports Object Oriented programming, it does not *require* it. Most experienced Python programmers (and programmers in general using a language that facilitates it) use `classes` and `polymorphism` relatively sparingly. There are a number of reasons why.

Most data that would otherwise stored in a `class` can be represented using the simple `list`, `dict`, and `set` types. Python has a wide variety of built-in functions and standard library modules optimized (both in design and implementation) to interact with them. One can make a compelling case that classes should be used only when necessary and almost never at API boundaries.

In Java, classes are the basic unit of encapsulation. Each file represents a Java class, regardless of whether that makes sense for the problem at hand. If I have a handful of utility functions, into a ``Utility'' class they go! If we don't intuitively understand what it means to be a ``Utility'' object, no matter. Of course, I exaggerate, but the point is clear. Once one is forced to make everything a class, it is easy to carry that notion over to other programming languages.

In Python, groups of related functions and data are naturally encapsulated in `modules`. If I'm using an MVC web framework to build ``Chirp'', I may have a package named `chirp` with `model`, `view`, and `controller` modules. If ``Chirp'' is an especially ambitious project and the code base is large, those modules could easily be `packages` themselves. The `controller` package may have a `persistence` module and a `processing` module. Neither of those need be related in any way other than the sense that they intuitively belong under `controller`.

If all of those modules became classes, interoperability immediately becomes an issue. We must carefully and precisely determine the methods we will expose publicly, how state will be updated, and the way in which our class supports testing. And instead of a `dict` or `list`, we have `Processing` and `Persistence` objects we must write code to support.

Note that nothing in the description of ``Chirp'' necessitates the use of any classes. Simple `import` statements make code sharing and encapsulation easy. Passing state explicitly as arguments to functions keeps everything loosely coupled. And it becomes far easier to receive, process, and transform data flowing through our system.

To be sure, classes may be a cleaner or more natural way to represent some ``things''. In many instances, `Object Oriented Programming` is a handy paradigm. Just don't make it the *only* paradigm you use.

3.5 Executable Scripts

3.5.1 Use the `if __name__ == '__main__'` pattern to allow a file to be both imported and run directly

Unlike the `main()` function available in some languages, Python has no built-in notion of a main entry point. Rather, the interpreter immediately begins executing statements upon loading a Python source file. If you want a file to function both as an importable Python module and a stand-alone script, use the `if __name__ == '__main__'` idiom.

3.5.1.1 Harmful

```python
import sys
import os

FIRST_NUMBER = float(sys.argv[1])
SECOND_NUMBER = float(sys.argv[2])


def divide(a, b):
    return a / b

# I can't import this file (for the super
# useful 'divide' function) without the following
# code being executed.
if SECOND_NUMBER != 0:
    print(divide(FIRST_NUMBER, SECOND_NUMBER))
```

3.5.1.2 Idiomatic

```python
import sys
import os


def divide(a, b):
    return a / b

# Will only run if script is executed directly,
# not when the file is imported as a module
if __name__ == '__main__':
    first_number = float(sys.argv[1])
```

```python
    second_number = float(sys.argv[2])
    if second_number != 0:
        print(divide(first_number, second_number))
```

3.5.2 Use `sys.exit` in your script to return proper error codes

Python scripts should be good shell citizens. It's tempting to jam a bunch of code after the if __name__ == '__main__' statement and not return anything. Avoid this temptation.

Create a main function that contains the code to be run as a script. Use `sys.exit` in main to return error codes if something goes wrong or zero if everything runs to completion. The only code under the if __name__ == '__main__' statement should call `sys.exit` with the return value of your main function as the parameter.

By doing this, we allow the script to be used in Unix pipelines, to be monitored for failure without needing custom rules, and to be called by other programs safely.

3.5.2.1 Harmful

```python
if __name__ == '__main__':
    import sys

    # What happens if no argument is passed on the
    # command line?
    if len(sys.argv) > 1:
        argument = sys.argv[1]
        result = do_stuff(argument)
        # Again, what if this is False? How would other
        # programs know?
        if result:
            do_stuff_with_result(result)
```

3.5.2.2 Idiomatic

```python
def main():
    import sys
    if len(sys.argv) < 2:
        # Calling sys.exit with a string automatically
        # prints the string to stderr and exits with
        # a value of '1' (error)
        sys.exit('You forgot to pass an argument')
    argument = sys.argv[1]
    result = do_stuff(argument)
    if not result:
```

```
        sys.exit(1)
        # We can also exit with just the return code

    do_stuff_with_result(result)

    # Optional, since the return value without this return
    # statment would default to None, which sys.exit treats
    # as 'exit with 0'
    return 0

# The three lines below are the canonical script entry
# point lines. You'll see them often in other Python scripts
if __name__ == '__main__':
        sys.exit(main())
```

Chapter 4

General Advice

4.1   Avoid Reinventing the Wheel

4.1.1   Get to know **PyPI** (the Python Package Index)

If Python's standard library doesn't have a package relevant to your particular problem, the chances are good that PyPI does. As of this writing, there are over **27,000** packages maintained in the index. If you're looking to accomplish a particular task and can't find a relevant package in PyPI, chances are it doesn't exist.

The index is fully searchable and contains both Python 2 and Python 3 based packages. Of course, not all packages are created equal (or equally maintained), so be sure to check when the package was last updated. A package with documentation hosted externally on a site like ReadTheDocs is a good sign, as is one for which the source is available on a site like GitHub or Bitbucket.

Now that you found a promising looking package, how do you install it? By far the most popular tool to manage third party packages is pip. A simple `pip install <package name>` will download the latest version of the package and install it in your `site-packages` directory. If you need the bleeding edge version of a package, `pip` is also capable of installing directly from a DVCS like `git` or `mercurial`.

If you create a package that seems generally useful, strongly consider giving back to the Python community by publishing it to PyPI. Doing so is a straightforward process, and future developers will (hopefully) thank you.

4.1.2　Learn the Contents of the Python Standard Library

Part of writing idiomatic code is making liberal use of the standard library. Code that unknowingly reimplements functionality in the standard library is perhaps the clearest signal of a novice Python programmer. Python is commonly said to come with ``batteries included'' for a good reason. The standard library contains packages covering a wide range of domains.

Making use of the standard library has two primary benefits. Most obviously, you save yourself a good deal of time when you don't have to implement a piece of functionality from scratch. Just as important is the fact that those who read or maintain your code will have a much easier time doing so if you use packages familiar to them.

Remember, the purpose of learning and writing idiomatic Python is to write clear, maintainable, and bug-free code. Nothing ensures those qualities in your code more easily than reusing code written and maintained by core Python developers. As bugs are found and fixed in the standard library, your code improves with each Python release without you lifting a finger.

4.2 Modules of Note

4.2.1 Learn the contents of the itertools module

If you frequent sites like StackOverflow, you may notice that the answer to questions of the form ``Why doesn't Python have the following obviously useful library function?'' almost always references the `itertools` module. The functional programming stalwarts that `itertools` provides should be seen as fundamental building blocks. What's more, the documentation for `itertools` has a `Recipes' section that provides idiomatic implementations of common functional programming constructs, all created using the itertools module. For some reason, a vanishingly small number of Python developers seem to be aware of the `Recipes' section and, indeed, the `itertools` module in general (hidden gems in the Python documentation is actually a recurring theme). Part of writing idiomatic code is knowing when you're reinventing the wheel.

4.2.2 Use functions in the `os.path` module when working with directory paths

When writing simple command-line scripts, new Python programmers often perform herculean feats of string manipulation to deal with file paths. Python has an entire module dedicated to functions on path names: `os.path`. Using `os.path` reduces the risk of common errors, makes your code portable, and makes your code much easier to understand.

4.2.2.1 Harmful

```python
from datetime import date
import os

filename_to_archive = 'test.txt'
new_filename = 'test.bak'
target_directory = './archives'
today = date.today()
os.mkdir('./archives/' + str(today))
os.rename(
    filename_to_archive,
    target_directory + '/' + str(today) + '/' + new_filename)
```

4.2.2.2 Idiomatic

```python
from datetime import date
import os

current_directory = os.getcwd()
filename_to_archive = 'test.txt'
new_filename = os.path.splitext(filename_to_archive)[0] + '.bak'
target_directory = os.path.join(current_directory, 'archives')
today = date.today()
new_path = os.path.join(target_directory, str(today))
if (os.path.isdir(target_directory)):
    if not os.path.exists(new_path):
        os.mkdir(new_path)
    os.rename(
        os.path.join(current_directory, filename_to_archive),
        os.path.join(new_path, new_filename))
```

4.3 Testing

4.3.1 Use an automated testing tool; it doesn't matter which one

Having automated tests is important for a variety of reasons (some of which are discussed in detail later in this chapter). Developers who haven't used automated testing tools often spend a great deal of time worrying about which tool to use. This is understandable, but usually not an issue. What *is* important is that you *actually use an automated testing tool (any of them)* and learn its functionality.

For most, the standard library's `unittest` module will be sufficient. It's a fully featured and reasonably user-friendly testing framework modeled after JUnit. Most of Python's standard library is tested using `unittest`, so it is quite capable of testing reasonably large and complex projects. Among other things, it includes:

- Automated test discovery
- Object-oriented resources for creating test cases and test suites
- An easy to use command line interface
- Ability to selectively enable/disable a subset of tests

If you find the `unittest` module lacking in functionality or writing test code not as intuitive as you'd like, there are a number of third-party tools available. The two most popular are `nose` and `py.test`, both freely available on PyPI. Both are actively maintained and extend the functionality offered by `unittest`.

If you decide to use one of them, choosing which is largely a matter of support for the functionality required by your project. Otherwise, it's mostly a matter of taste regarding the style of test code each packaged supports. This book, for example, has used both tools at various points of its development, switching based on changing test requirements.

When you do make a decision, even if it's to use the `unittest` module, familiarize yourself with all of the capabilities of the tool you chose. Each have a long list of useful features. The more you take advantage of these features, the less time you'll spend inadvertently implementing a feature which you weren't aware the tool you use already supports.

4.3.2   Separate your test code from your application code

When writing test code, some developers are tempted to include it in the same module as the code it's meant to test. This is typically done by including test classes or functions in the same file as the code to be tested and relying on test discovery tools to run them. A (thankfully) less common alternative is to use the `if __name__ == '__main__'` idiom to run test code when the module is invoked directly.

There's no good reason to shoehorn test code and application code into the same file, but there are a number of reasons not to. The documentation on Python's `unittest` module succinctly enumerates these, so I'll simply list their reasons here:

- The test module can be run standalone from the command line.
- The test code can more easily be separated from shipped code.
- There is less temptation to change test code to fit the code it tests without a good reason.
- Test code should be modified much less frequently than the code it tests.
- Tested code can be refactored more easily.
- Tests for modules written in C must be in separate modules anyway, so why not be consistent?
- If the testing strategy changes, there is no need to change the source code.

As a general rule, if the official Python documentation strongly suggests something, it can safely be considered idiomatic Python.

4.3.3   Use unit tests to aid in refactoring

Idiomatic Python code is terse and easy to read. Python developers are accustomed to getting results quickly without the need to give much thought to the organization of code. This is great for rapid prototyping and short scripts, but any non-trivial piece of software will likely be *refactored* many times throughout its lifetime.

To *refactor* code is to restructure it without changing its observable behavior. Imagine we have a function that calculates various statistics about students' test scores and outputs the results in nicely-formatted HTML. This single function might be *refactored* into two smaller functions: one to perform the calculations and the other to print the results as HTML. After the refactoring, the resulting HTML output will be the same as before, but the structure of the code itself was changed to increase readability. Refactoring is a deep topic and a full discussion is outside the scope of this book, but it's likely something you'll find yourself doing often.

As you're making changes, though, how do you know if you've inadvertently broken something? And how do you know which portion of code is responsible for the bug? Automated unit testing is your canary in the mine shaft of refactoring. It's an early warning system that lets you know something has gone wrong. Catching bugs quickly is important; the sooner you catch a bug, the easier it is to fix.

Unit tests are the specific type of tests helpful for this purpose. A unit test is different from other types of tests in that it tests small portions of code in isolation. Unit tests may be written against functions, classes, or entire modules, but they test the behavior of the code in question *and no more*. Thus, if the code makes database queries or network connections, these are simulated in a controlled way by *mocking* those resources. The goal is to be absolutely sure that, if a test fails, it's because of the code being tested and not due to some unrelated code or resource.

It should be clear, then, how unit tests are helpful while refactoring. Since only the internal structure of the code is changing, tests that examine the code's output should still pass. If such a test fails, it means that the refactoring introduced unintended behavior. Sometimes you'll need to make changes to your tests themselves, of course, depending on the scope of the code changes you're making. In general, though, passing unit tests is a good litmus test for determining if your refactoring broke anything.

Lastly, your unit tests should be *automated* so that running them and interpreting the results requires no thought on your part. Just kick off the tests and make sure all the tests still pass. If you need to manually run specific tests based on what part of the system you're changing, you run the risk of running the wrong tests or missing a bug introduced in a portion of the code you didn't intend to affect (and thus didn't test). Like most developer productivity tools, the purpose is to reduce the cognitive burden on the developer and increase reliability and repeatability.

Chapter 5

Contributors

I actively solicit feedback on bugs, typos, grammatical and spelling errors, and unclear portions of the text. The following **awesome** individuals have greatly helped improve the quality of this text by emailing me about an issue they found.

- R. Daneel Olivaw
- Jonathon Capps
- Michael G. Lerner
- Daniel Smith
- Arne Sellmann
- Nick Van Hoogenstyn
- Kiran Gangadharan
- Brian Brechbuhl
- Mike White
- Brandon Devine
- Johannes Krampf
- Marco Kaulea

Index

www.ingramcontent.com/pod-product-compliance
Lightning Source LLC
Chambersburg PA
CBHW041421050326
40689CB00002B/594